Bitcoin and Blockchain for Beginners

The Complete Guide to Investing in Bitcoin and Understanding Blockchain Cryptocurrency for Complete Beginners (2022)

Ollie Ruell

Introduction

As cryptocurrencies such as Bitcoin gained popularity worldwide, the term "blockchain" has emerged from obscurity and into the spotlight, thanks to a significant increase in coverage from mainstream media outlets.

"Blockchain" has even become a bit of a buzzword in the tech and finance sectors, as well as in a growing number of other fields and industries.

The term "blockchain" has received a lot of attention recently, but what exactly does it mean? What exactly is blockchain technology?

What exactly does it do? How does it function? What is the significance of this? These questions are not often handled with due diligence in the stream of headlines and "thought pieces" about digital currencies and other blockchain-based applications. As a result, many individuals have imperfect knowledge of this disruptive new technology and its future implications.

One difficulty in learning about blockchains is that much of the true power behind the scenes of this technology includes sophisticated mathematical operations that can be difficult to grasp for those of us without extensive degrees in computer science or a background in cryptography.

Unless you intend to become a developer and create your blockchain applications, you may obtain a complete understanding of how blockchains operate on a practical level without having to deal with any algorithms.

The purpose of this book is not to delve into the mathematical wizardry needed to develop blockchain-based applications but rather to serve as an introduction to the broader architecture and conceptual foundations of blockchain technology.

We'll take a hands-on approach, looking at how blockchains are utilized in the real world, how they operate, and why many vital voices worldwide are hailing this technology as revolutionary.

When the Internet came along, it completely changed the organization of daily life worldwide. Many people feel that the ramifications of blockchain technology will result in a similar-scale paradigm upheaval. Blockchain is a fundamental technology that can transform the character of institutions, industries, and the global economy.

However, before we set the world on fire, let's go over the fundamentals: what is a blockchain, how does it function, and what exactly it does?

These are some of the core questions we will attempt to answer throughout this book.

However, before we begin to investigate this futuristic technology, it is helpful first to understand its history.

Where did the concept of Blockchain originate?

Table of content

CHAPTER 1

Conclusion

CHAPTER 1

A Quick Overview of Blockchain

Technology

Satoshi Nakamoto created the concept of a "blockchain" in 2008 as part of the technology behind the digital currency Bitcoin.

Nakamoto sent a technical paper to a popular email list for cryptography enthusiasts that laid out the fundamental ideas of Bitcoin, a digital currency, and the Blockchain, the underlying technology powering that money.

Shortly after, in 2009, the first Blockchain was put into action when Nakamoto mined and distributed the first Bitcoin. Today, Bitcoin has earned global acclaim and is accepted as good money by an increasing number of merchants. Bitcoin may be used to purchase anything from airline tickets to online courses; even Burger King has begun to accept it!

Many different digital currencies, sometimes referred to as "cryptocurrencies," have evolved during the last decade, all of which use blockchain technology to manage transactions. Some of them will be discussed in later chapters of this book. Still, it is crucial to remember that the implications of blockchain technology extend far beyond the domain of digital currency.

While cryptocurrencies, notably Bitcoin, were the first to use blockchains, many businesses are now investigating blockchain technology as a mechanism to handle a wide range of procedures, including smart contracts, data storage, and resource management. Throughout this book, we will look at various ways that blockchain applications are being built, both for cryptocurrencies and in other sectors.

One of the more intriguing facts in the history of blockchain technology, anecdotally, is the name of its developer. Despite several theories, no one has ever discovered Satoshi Nakamoto's genuine identity.

We may never know whether Nakamoto is one human or a group of people. What is known is that their contribution to the future of technology will be enormous. With good reason, many notable thinkers and voices in the computer world consider blockchain technology as having revolutionary potential

CHAPTER 2

Blockchain Fundamentals

Managing Digital Transactions

Various underlying notions make blockchain technology particularly well-suited to digital transactions. The most well-known and commonly used application of blockchains today is in the cryptocurrency industry, where blockchains are used to conduct financial transactions that take place digitally on a peer-to-peer basis.

While blockchain technology's applications are not restricted to digital financial transactions, this is a fantastic location to start learning about how blockchains function in practice. Digital currencies, led by Bitcoin, have developed as a new asset class in and of itself, which is extraordinary. Aside from the creation of digital assets, the blockchain architecture presents a model for rethinking institutional structures in terms of power organization and value distribution. We are still in the early phases of investigating the possibilities of blockchain technology, but the field is rapidly evolving. It is not an exaggeration to say that blockchain technology will radically alter the structure of governments, personal property, and the global economy within the next decade.

To acquire a better understanding of how blockchains function, consider looking at digital currencies such as Bitcoin. As of now, digital currencies are the most well-established implementations of functional blockchains.

Blockchain technology is used to conduct financial transactions in the case of digital currencies, or "cryptocurrencies." Before we look at how the blockchain model works, it is helpful to understand how financial transactions have historically operated.

Financial Transactions and How We Handle Them

For generations, people have relied on centralized organizations like banks and governments to function as mediators in storing and exchanging financial assets.

In practice, most people maintain the majority of their finances in a bank. There are numerous advantages to doing so. If, for example, you had your entire life savings buried beneath your house's floorboards and your home burned down, you'd be in huge trouble.

Banks promise protection by safeguarding your funds in exchange for various transaction fees. We trust banks to keep our savings safe in exchange for a percentage of our money. This approach of storing money in banks became the standard over time. However, in an increasingly digital environment, many people have begun to seek alternatives to the historical model of consolidating resources in centralized organizations.

As more and more transactions are conducted digitally, the requirement for trust and security is becoming increasingly important. Financial data exists primarily as data, and transactions are essentially just filed transfers. It is pretty simple to modify data without a safe method.

Hackers frequently breach bank systems, ATM machines, and other locations where financial data is stored or transactions take place.

One of the most challenging aspects of handling financial transactions on a peer-to-peer basis is preventing "double-spending," or ensuring that someone does not spend the same money again. When Bitcoin first appeared on the market, it provided a solution to this problem by allowing direct peer-to-peer transactions to take place in a safe manner that did not require trust from either party or a third-party middleman, such as a bank. The Blockchain was that solution.

What exactly is a Distributed Ledger?

While Bitcoin pioneered blockchain technology, many additional applications, including but not limited to other digital currencies, have been built on it. The usage of a distributed ledger system is one of the core concepts driving the success of blockchain technology.

So, what exactly is a distributed ledger? A distributed ledger is, in essence, precisely what it sounds like. A ledger is simply a list of records; instead of storing it in a single location, a distributed ledger simultaneously keeps it in multiple locations. Although not all distributed ledgers are blockchains, all blockchains use some sort of distributed ledger.

One of the fundamental concepts underlying Blockchain is decentralization.

The requirement for a "trusted" third party institution to serve as a middleman and oversee transactions is eliminated by keeping several copies of the record of transactions in different locations all over the world, viewable to anybody.

To better understand how distributed ledgers work, consider the following scenario: Assume you have a large three-ring binder in which you record every financial transaction you make in a year.

Every time you make or spend money, you record the data in this binder. There is only one binder, which you keep on your desk.

In this scenario, a lot of things may go wrong: your house could burn down, a malevolent individual could sneak in and tamper with the data, you could forget to include a few documents and wind up with figures that don't add up, or any number of other unpleasant mishaps.

Instead of having just one binder, imagine hundreds of thousands of identical copies of the same binder in people's desks worldwide. Every time a new detail was added to the binder, it had to be checked against all of the copies to ensure that the numbers were added up correctly, and the latest information had to be added into all of them at once. If a binder containing a transaction that did not appear in any of the others, we could conclude that the binder was defective.

To tamper with your data, someone would have to fiddle with every single one of these binders all over the world at the same time. Using a binder system on desks is obviously impractical.

However, this is fairly analogous to how a distributed ledger operates in the virtual world. No matter how large or small, each unique transaction is recorded in a "block" on blockchains.

Each block has a unique timestamp that connects it to the previous block. This enables computers to compare each proposed transaction against the prior one. The transaction will be refused if the timestamps do not add up correctly across most computers. If the majority approves the proposed transaction, it will be confirmed and added to a new block in the chain or a new record in the ledger. Now, the following proposed transaction will be compared to the timestamp of that block, and so on.

To input false information into the Blockchain, someone, such as a hacker, would have to change the information not only on one block but on every single block on the whole Blockchain at the same time, across the majority of participating computers all over the world. Even with today's technology, accomplishing that would necessitate such vast amounts of computing power that it would be essentially unattainable. As a result, the distributed ledger system of the Blockchain is secure by design.

Because each transaction is reviewed against the whole history of prior transactions by numerous machines dispersed throughout the world, it is impossible to "cheat" the Blockchain by attempting to spend the same money twice. One of the transactions will be rejected as invalid since it does not match the historical record.

Not only is the problem of "double spending" eliminated, but transactions no longer require either side to trust the other or a third-party institution to be completed. Person A cannot claim that they sent money to Person B that "went missing in the mail," and Person B cannot claim they "never received the money."

Because all transactions are public, both parties will be able to see a record of the transaction on the Blockchain.

Bitcoin and Blockchain

When we attempt to decouple the Blockchain from Bitcoin, we encounter one of the concept's most perplexing and misunderstood parts.

As previously noted, Bitcoin is merely one application built on a blockchain infrastructure. It is also the world's first, largest, and most well-known operational open blockchain. Bitcoin's application of blockchain technology is frequently considered as definitive, which means that when people say "blockchain," they are frequently referring to the blockchain model utilized by Bitcoin.

It is critical to recognize that the Bitcoin model is not the only way to use blockchain technology. Bitcoin is one example of this technology in action.

Several factors contribute to Bitcoin's blockchain functioning as it does, and it is worthwhile to investigate each of them to gain a better understanding of which aspects of Bitcoin's blockchain implementation are unique to Bitcoin and which are aspects of blockchain technology in general.

Bitcoin's Blockchain

Several fundamental concepts interact to form a blockchain ecosystem that is unique to Bitcoin. Other cryptocurrencies have used similar ideas, but we'll focus on Bitcoin and examine how the Bitcoin blockchain works for our purposes.

Blockchains are already known to be a type of distributed ledger. If we delve a little deeper into the concept of a distributed ledger, various problems may arise, such as:

- how are transactions verified?
- Who keeps track of them?
- How can we be sure that this information is correct?

Encryption

If you recall from the previous section on the history of Bitcoin, the notion was first introduced to a popular cryptography email group. Why is cryptography used?

As a means of safeguarding information, the field of cryptography has grown fast alongside digital technology. Cryptography has long been a rather arcane field, employed primarily on military circumstances. Julius Cesar famously utilized encryption technology to convey coded communications to his generals during the Roman Empire.

Encryption has become an essential component of daily life in the digital age.

As hacking and identity theft has become more prevalent, simple encryption methods have entered the mainstream as preventative measures for safeguarding one's data. Most of us today are already familiar with simple encryption strategies, such as using passwords to access our email accounts or enabling two-factor authentication on our cellphones, whether we realize it or not. From making online purchases to accessing our bank accounts, most of us rely on encrypted transactions regularly.

So it's no surprise that Bitcoin relies on cryptographically secure methods to validate transactions and manage the Blockchain

CHAPTER 3

The Hashing Algorithm

SHA-256

Bitcoin employs a cryptographically secure hashing algorithm known as SHA-256. While an in-depth explanation of how this works is beyond the scope of this book, a basic overview is helpful. Imagine a black box as one way to think about this. The SHA-256 algorithm is represented by the box. We won't be concerned with what happens within the box, the nuts and bolts of the algorithm itself for our purposes. We'll just go with the assumption that mysterious mathematical things happen inside the box.

The critical aspect for us is that you can feed any type of data, of any size, into the box. Ultimately, all digital data exists as a sequence of 1's and 0's, or "bits," even complicated objects like movies that are many gigabytes in size. When we input any type of data into the SHA-256 black box, the bits in that data are processed. Inside the box, the bits can be thought of as being "rearranged." When the black box processes the data, it sends out a 256-bit stream of seemingly random characters that appears to be nonsense. Consider this string to be a one-of-a-kind "fingerprint" of the data we entered.

(The data, in this case, is the word "hello" hashed with SHA-256)

To be honest, the apparent "nonsense" that comes out is not nonsense. SHA-256 is determinative, which means that if you feed the same data into the "black box," you will always get the exact identical output string, or "fingerprint."

If you use SHA-256 on the word "hello," you will obtain the exact 64-character string as seen above.

Another distinguishing property of this hash function is that it is one-way. This means that you cannot transform the output string back to the original data. So, in our example, we can't go back to the initial "hello" by utilizing the "nonsense."

One application for this is to validate documents, such as PDFs. If you sign a contract and give it to someone along with the SHA-256 fingerprint, they can verify that not a single bit of the data has been altered. If they run the document via SHA-256 and get the same return string, the document has not been modified.

If, on the other hand, even the most minor change has occurred - whether it was a well-intentioned update like fixing a typo or a case of criminal interference - the fingerprint that emerges will be radically different.

The algorithm is unconcerned with the nature or extent of the alteration to the original data; the result of the SHA-256 method will be completely different unless the data is 100 percent identical. For example, in the preceding example, changing the word "hello" to "Hello" or "HELLO" results in a completely different output string.

You may be wondering how this connects to the Bitcoin blockchain now that we have a basic understanding of how SHA-256 works. This is one of the more difficult things to grasp when it comes to what happens under the hood of Bitcoin's system. To understand the importance of SHA-256 in the "Proof of Work" model that allows Bitcoin to work, we must first look at how Bitcoin miners interact in the blockchain ecosystem.

The Function of Bitcoin Miners

Many descriptions of how Bitcoin transactions are validated state that "miners solve complex math problems to add blocks to the chain in exchange for a reward."

This is correct, and it is a good explanation for comprehending the big picture. However, when it comes to an understanding the overall architecture of blockchain technology as it applies to Bitcoin, we find that this explanation is a little oversimplified. For our needs, we need to dig a little deeper into the mechanics of Bitcoin mining.

Mining entails doing complex computations in order to find specific combinations of random integers (known as "nonces"). These nonces are paired with information about specific Bitcoin transactions to produce an SHA-256 string that passes extremely stringent standards.

The header, or first "chunk," of any block on the Blockchain contains data on Bitcoin transactions, which is shown as an SHA-256 string. As a result, the first "chunk" of the string that makes up each block contains information on the transactions in that block, such as the time, amount of Bitcoin involved, addresses involved, and other details.

The remainder of the string is generated by locating a nonce that, when combined with the transaction data, results in an SHA-256 string that matches the aforementioned target criteria.

So, what are the criteria, and who makes the decision? Bitcoin blocks must be built in accordance with a set of rules to be accepted by the consensus model that governs all "nodes" on the Bitcoin network. This rule set—the conditions that must be followed in order to generate a valid block—is written into the Bitcoin software's core code. The "rules" are a collection of functions written into C++ code that runs on every system (or "node") connected to the Bitcoin network.

A miner must follow these requirements when creating a block. To begin, the block must contain information about the most recent Bitcoin transactions. The miner must then find a nonce that, when combined with the transaction data, produces a SHA-256 string that matches the standards specified by Bitcoin's software (for example, the criteria might be something like the string must contain 15 zeroes in a row).

There is no other way to find the nonce than to use "brute force," which essentially means trial and error. Miners try a large number of random numbers in a short period of time until they locate one that works.

When a miner "solves a block," they have discovered a nonce that generates a SHA-256 hash that matches the criteria for a legitimate block. They can then publish their solution to the Bitcoin network, where other nodes will validate it.

To give you an idea of how difficult it is to find the nonce, consider that the Bitcoin network generates up to 500 quadrillion hashes each second. All of these are attempts to find a nonce that gives the desired result. Even with that tremendous amount of work, solving a block or finding a suitable nonce takes an average of 10 minutes.

When a miner successfully solves a block, they are rewarded with a small amount of Bitcoin.

Satoshi Nakamoto's Bitcoin

(http://bitcoin.org/bitcoin.pdf),

MIT,

https://commons.wikimedia.org/w/index.php?curid=24542868

(The term "Merkle Root" refers to a mathematical construct known as a Merkle Tree.) The Merkle Root in this situation is the hash of all the transactions in the block. Each individual transaction's information are also hashed, therefore the "Merkle Root" is the hash of all of those hashes.)

Bitcoin miners are required to pay in order to participate.

You may have heard of Bitcoin mining as a means to earn "free money." This was never the case, even in the early days of Bitcoin, and it is even less true today, since the complexity of solving blocks increases over time in direct proportion to the amount of Bitcoin in circulation.

The specificity of the SHA-256 string increases over time (this is known as the "difficulty goal"), increasing the amount of power required to find a valid nonce. Today, specific equipment is required to mine Bitcoin in any meaningful way, and even then, most miners pool their resources to share both the burden of work and the profits.

Miners utilize their equipment to test hashes at breakneck speed. As you might expect, this level of computational power necessitates a significant amount of electricity, which is not always free. The Bitcoin mining infrastructure works in part because miners must pay to participate. There is no reward without the sacrifice. Someone will only mine Bitcoin if they believe the incentive is worth more than the substantial electric expenditure that mining incurs.

When a miner discovers a working nonce, their result is verified and validated by the Bitcoin network as a whole. If everything checks up, they have given Proof of Work and are eligible for their prize. If the rest of the nodes on the Bitcoin network notice that something in a proposed block does not meet the criteria, either by following a rule incorrectly or by failing to provide a nonce that meets the criteria, the block will be rejected, and the miner's money and resources will have been wasted. For example, if someone tries to "double-spend," the effort will be detected and the block will be refused.

Because Bitcoin employs a Proof-of-Work consensus architecture, it is nearly hard to cheat or hack the Blockchain. Miners pay to play with Bitcoin, and it only pays to play fairly. Not only that, but those who do not play fairly will lose money due to the high cost of electricity required to run mining rigs.

Blockchain Extending Beyond Bitcoin

When we examine the Bitcoin Blockchain, we can see that it is composed of multiple unique pieces that work together to form the overall architecture of the ecosystem. So far, we've looked at three components: the concept of a distributed ledger, the use of SHA-256, and a cryptographic key. Consensus model based on Proof-of-Work.

Which of these are unique to Bitcoin, and which are inherent in the concept of blockchain technology itself? That's an excellent question, and the answer may vary depending on who you ask. There is some disagreement about where Bitcoin ends and Blockchain begins or what properties of Bitcoin's Blockchain are required to create additional blockchains that work in a practical sense.

When we remove the trappings of Bitcoin from the fundamental concept of a blockchain, we are ultimately left with the notion of a distributed ledger containing a record of transactions.

Different blockchain applications may handle different types of transactions and how they are handled, confirmed, and recorded.

When we start looking into various blockchain implementations, we need to pay close attention to how they work. How do they ensure safety? Are they open and accessible to the public? Do they have a decentralized system? How are they encrypting data? Are the transactions private? What kind of transactions are handled? Do they make use of Proof of Work? Is there another paradigm of agreement? All of these problems arise when we consider blockchain technology in contexts other than Bitcoin

CHAPTER 4

Bitcoin Isn't the Only

Cryptocurrency

Ethereum

The cryptocurrency market is infamous for its volatility. Things change on a daily basis, and new coins are always being generated. What is groundbreaking one day may become antiquated the next. Having said that, there are several digital currencies that have acquired some degree of stability. Although Bitcoin is commonly regarded as the market leader in blockchain-based currencies,

Ethereum has garnered significant traction since its debut in late 2013.

Vitalik Buterin, a programmer, created Ethereum. Unlike Bitcoin, which only operates as a digital money, Ethereum is a blockchain-based platform for creating decentralized apps that use "smart contracts." Whereas Bitcoin functions as a peer-to-peer electronic cash system, the Ethereum blockchain runs the code that makes up decentralized applications.

It may be useful to think of Ethereum in terms of a smartphone. A smartphone includes a generic operating system, such as iOS or Android. Anyone can design apps that accomplish a variety of tasks and run on that operating system. In this comparison, Ethereum is like the operating system: a foundation upon which to build.

One application that runs on Ethereum is a digital currency known colloquially as "Ethereum," while technically it is known as Ether.

This can be perplexing because both the currency and the platform are commonly referred to as "Ethereum," but it's vital to realize that the currency is only one component of the Ethereum blockchain infrastructure. Ethereum "miners" are compensated with Ether as a reward for maintaining the Ethereum blockchain.

Ethereum mining has used a Proof-of-Work consensus approach, similar to Bitcoin, since its creation. However, as of 2017, the Ethereum team revealed plans to switch to a Proof-of-Stake mechanism. Understanding the distinction between these two methods of authenticating blockchain transactions is critical for providing context for some of today's most important concerns in the greater blockchain environment.

When we discussed "Proof of Work" as an essential component of the Bitcoin protocol, we discussed how Bitcoin miners must invest in expensive mining equipment that consumes a lot of electricity in order to solve a block. Proof-of-Stake (PoS) operates in a unique manner.

A Proof-of-Stake mechanism is more akin to gambling. Ethereum is shifting away from the word "miners" and toward the term "validators." Validators put their own money (Ether, in the case of Ethereum) on the line to solve a block. The more money a validator stakes, the more likely it is that they will solve the block.

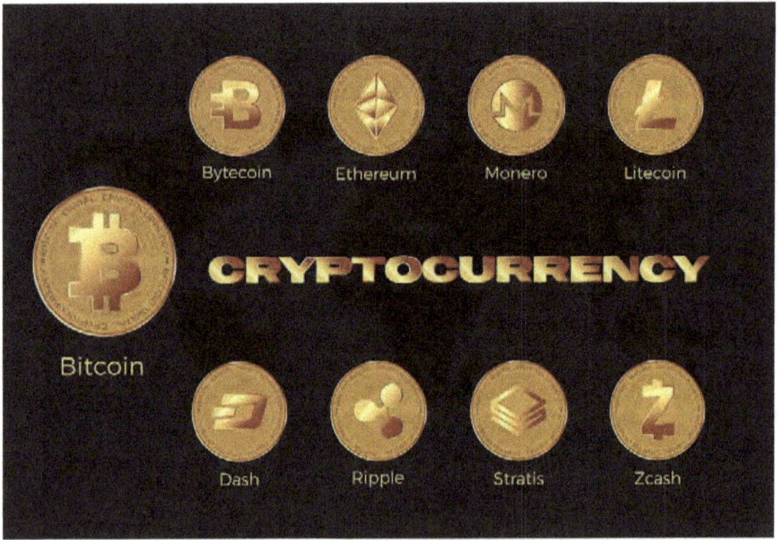

In this case, four validators are "staking" their own money on the solution of a block. Validator 4 has the biggest stake, and hence the highest chance of completing the puzzle and being rewarded.

The Proof-of-Stake concept simulates the "labour" required in completing meaningless computations, reducing the true environmental impact of mining's energy use. We know that validators risk their money on solving a block, much like a gambler, but what happens if someone tries to "cheat"?

In Ethereum's Proof-of-Stake mechanism (named Casper), in the event of a bad actor, the funds belonging to anyone attempting to do something evil will just vanish! They will be removed from circulation by the system. As a result, the incentive for a validator to engage in earnest is considerable, as are the consequences of attempting to "verify" a fake transaction.

Both the Proof-of-Work and Proof-of-Stake models ultimately seek the same result: they aim to validate blocks and add them to the Blockchain in such a way that the broader network agrees on the validity of those blocks. Both models should, ideally, achieve the same outcome via a separate procedure.

As a potential investor or player in the blockchain field, familiarising yourself with various consensus models is a smart method to gain a better grasp of how projects work in practice. The transition of Ethereum's model from Proof-of-Work based on mining to Proof-of-Stake based on validation will further distinguish Ethereum from Bitcoin in terms of structure, but it is also worth considering some of the other ways in which these two technologies are already fundamentally quite different.

As previously said, Ethereum, while partially a currency, is principally a platform for developing decentralized apps.

The concept of decentralized applications (also known as "dApps") can be a little perplexing, owing to the fact that it is a whole new way of organizing information. Why do we require a blockchain-based platform for application development? This is a question for which many programmers are still looking for answers. One answer, though, has to do with a concept known as "state" in the programming world.

The term "state" simply refers to the current status of any specific application or programme. One feature that distinguishes Ethereum's Blockchain from Bitcoin's is that "transactions" on the Ethereum blockchain can actually cause code to be run. As a result, programmes can be triggered to run as a result of transactions on the Ethereum platform. When something changes within an application, the state of that application changes. Every state change that occurs within an application is recorded on the Ethereum blockchain.

A smart contract, for example, can be paid when work is completed entirely on the Ethereum blockchain.

Don't worry if you're feeling a little lost. You don't need to comprehend the technical details of state change unless you plan on developing applications on the Ethereum platform. Having said that, if you intend to get involved in the blockchain area as an investor or entrepreneur, it is worthwhile to become acquainted with these principles. Let's have a look at one of the decentralized apps being developed on the Ethereum platform to get a better picture of what Ethereum is capable of.

- **Golem**

Golem is a well-known project built on the Ethereum architecture. The concept is straightforward. Many people own computers. Many people who own computers do not use them all of the time, and even when they do, they frequently do not use them to their full processing capabilities. Simultaneously, there are several industries where huge quantities of processing power are necessary to do particular tasks. Rendering video, for example, is quite expensive in terms of CPU power. It takes a long time, and it can be rather slow on a slow machine. Many scientific research necessitates computationally expensive data analysis and other types of high-level computer processing.

The Golem project is intended to allow users to rent out their unused computer processing power to people who require it for projects. Because of the decentralized structure, people from all over the world can contribute little amounts of computer power to completing a computationally complex task that would normally require a highly powerful computer to complete.

Golem is trying to create what are basically decentralized supercomputers that are accessible to anybody by utilizing a blockchain-based framework that allows code to be executed when transactions occur, i.e., Ethereum. Because the Ethereum blockchain records the complete history of a program's state, participants can ensure that no one is utilizing more power than they have paid for and vice versa, as well as other characteristics surrounding their transactions.

Golem also has its own digital currency, based on Ether, via which participants can buy and sell resources and, of course, in which anybody can invest whether or not they are directly involved in the project. As of this writing, Golem is largely regarded as one of the more popular and successful applications created on the Ethereum platform.

- **Ripple**

We've already discussed some of the differences between Ethereum and Bitcoin. One thing we haven't mentioned yet is that, unlike Bitcoin, Ethereum is administered by a centralized team of well-known individuals. This organization decides what occurs with Ethereum, such as the transition from Proof-of-Work to Proof-of-Stake, and so has more centralized control over the platform than Bitcoin. Nonetheless, Ethereum remains an open blockchain platform that anybody can use.

Ripple is another example of a blockchain-based variant. Ripple is two things: a cryptocurrency and a blockchain technology firm. Ripple's focus is on the financial industry as a whole, partnering with banks and financial institutions to implement blockchain technology into their infrastructure.

Ripple is still somewhat controversial among cryptocurrency aficionados, although it claims to alleviate some of Bitcoin's flaws. Ripple, most importantly, eliminates the verification waiting period. Transactions can occur in real-time. However, Ripple's consensus process differs from Bitcoin's "Proof of Work" concept, relying instead on a centralized network of "trusted" servers, raising serious concerns for people drawn to blockchain technology because of the promise of decentralized architecture.

The implementation of a distributed ledger with blockchain technology symbolizes a fundamental reworking of institutional organizations from a hierarchical model to a distributed network. For many investors, this is the key to unlocking blockchain technology's transformative potential. The ramifications of decentralizing information are profound, and they are almost certainly not fully appreciated.

CHAPTER 5

Blockchain's Implications

Big Data, Privacy, and Personal Data

As we approach a more digital age, many of the activities that existed previous to the Internet are merely being applied to the new framework of a networked world. For example, instead of writing letters, we now send emails. On the surface, the method does not appear to be all that different. It isn't always the case.

Whatever your feelings are, there is no denying that more and more things are being integrated onto the Internet, hence the aptly named concept of the "Internet of Things" (often abbreviated to IoT). Heart-rate monitors, self-driving cars, and even refrigerators are making their way to market. Of course, practically everyone is already used to carrying a smartphone with them at all times, checking GPS data, updating social media feeds, handling financial transactions, and much more.

Almost every aspect of life is either now connected to the Internet or will be in the near future. While the developing revolution in "smart technology" has many advantages, it also has some big issues and challenges. While it may appear like social media networks, smart toasters, and FitBits are all completely separate concepts, they actually have a lot in common. In essence, they all generate data: data on you. As we mentioned in the section on SHA-256, all digital data can eventually be converted to 0's and 1's. From that vantage point, our heart rate and our Google search history aren't all that dissimilar.

We are all continuously producing data, whether it is instructing Amazon's Alexa to get more paper towels, Googling photographs of young sea lions, or recording your gym programme with an App or a wearable.

Where does this information end up? Who owns this information? What may your data trail reveal about you? Anyone brave enough to ask these questions will shortly find themselves in extremely uncomfortable ground. While delving into the answers to these specific concerns is beyond the scope of this book, it is worthwhile to touch the surface. In a nutshell, massive multi-national corporations buy your data and sell it to other corporations. What are they going to do with it? That's an excellent question. Of course, they target advertising depending on your previous behavior. Sure. We're all aware of it. But what else is there? Part of what makes this path unsettling is that no one really knows, and the domain of data collection is ill-defined and poorly governed.

Let's have a look at an example. Let's pretend you discovered a small bump in your armpit one day. You're understandably scared, so you run over to Google and spend several hours browsing around different websites reading cancer stories. Let's imagine, theoretically, that whoever is sucking up your data gets their hands on this data-sucking spree. Perhaps they also see that you sought for a phone number for a local doctor who performs cancer screenings. While you're at it, perhaps it's time to reconsider your health insurance policy or acquire life insurance just in case?

Continuing the example, what would happen if an insurance provider bought your data, which had previously been analyzed by some big data broker, and discovered that you had lately looked up information about cancer? Even if you haven't told anybody about the lump, and you haven't been tested or diagnosed, may this possible insurer deduce things from your data history when deciding on your premium amount, or whether to offer you insurance at all?

This is only one of many ethical and legal quandaries that arise when we consider the ramifications of our data, how it is mined, who "owns" it, and who has access to it.

The stronger the integration of technology into society and all aspects of life and the pervasiveness of networks, the larger the volume and variety of data about all of us. What movies and music we stream, our shopping history, political leanings, sexual preferences, social network connections, devices we use, and much more are all examples of information that is frequently collected as a result of blindly checking a user agreement box in order to use a particular service.

Okay, that's creepy, but how does it relate to blockchain technology?

That's an excellent question. The link between privacy and technology is a topic that cuts across numerous businesses and current issues.

Privacy is a big worry for many cryptocurrencies and blockchain technology aficionados. When it comes to "privacy," many observers, including major media outlets, believe that "the only individuals who worry about privacy are those who have something to hide." This has resulted in a significant amount of reporting on cryptocurrencies, specifically, implying that the fundamental appeal of these technologies is that they facilitate illegal conduct. As more and more aspects of life become linked to the Internet, it is implausible to claim that wanting more control over one's personal data, transactions, and wealth management constitutes or suggests criminal behaviour. Many privacy supporters say that privacy is necessary for both individual well-being and a functioning democracy.

Rather than depending on centralized organizations to deliver services in exchange for data ownership, blockchain-based solutions that shift information to a secure, trustless, decentralized framework are emerging. ("Trustless" means that participants do not need to rely on a centralized organization to broker transactions, keep records, distribute wealth, store data, and so on.)

The implications of Blockchain in areas such as personal information management, such as health records, are incredibly promising and are gaining a lot of interest from investors, entrepreneurs, huge organizations, and government entities.

Regardless of your sentiments about privacy, it is worth noting from a financial standpoint that numerous significant cryptocurrencies have arisen with privacy as a defining element. The capacity to conduct completely anonymous and safe transactions has propelled several currencies to the forefront of the cryptocurrency field, including Monero, ZCash, and Dash. While none of these have achieved the widespread adoption of Bitcoin or Ethereum, all three are among the top 50 cryptocurrencies in terms of market value. We may deduce from their performance that enough individuals demand anonymity to make these currencies competitive players in the wider cryptocurrency market as well as the broader blockchain environment.

Taking Advantage of Blockchain Technologies

It is critical to remember that blockchain technology is still in its infancy. The ramifications of this type of secure distributed ledgers and decentralized peer-to-peer systems are still being explored. There are several opportunities in the digital arena, as there are in any frontier space. Of course, the essence of frontiers is that they are uncharted territory, and where there is opportunity, there is also a higher risk element than one may experience in calmer and more controlled areas.

While much of the blockchain market is still in its infancy, prominent companies and industry leaders from a variety of industries are beginning to invest in and investigate blockchain technology. Blockchains are being investigated by major technology companies such as IBM and Microsoft and numerous banks, particularly in Europe and Asia.

Many governments around the world are starting to use blockchains to handle public services and data. Estonia, for example, provides residents with cryptographically secure ID cards that are controlled by a blockchain and offer access to a variety of public services. The Georgian government is implementing blockchain technology to handle land titles and confirm property transactions.

The United Nations recently completed a pilot initiative to coordinate the distribution of food aid to 10,000 refugees using the Ethereum blockchain.

Many hedge funds dealing in cryptocurrencies and blockchain applications have sprung up all over the world in recent years, and many Wall Street speculators have focused their attention on the blockchain industry. Overstock, one of the largest online merchants in the United States, launched a blockchain-based platform for equities trading in 2016. A slew of firms has sprung up that use blockchains to administer peer-to-peer micropayments at incredibly low rates. In some circumstances, this allow for international transfers and cash pickups, allowing unbanked individuals to make and receive money.

In the blockchain realm, new advancements occur daily. Staying educated is the single most crucial thing you can do if you want to dive in, become involved, and profit from these rising technologies: Read white papers, participate in online communities, and learn about the various blockchain-related projects that are gaining traction. The more knowledgeable you are with the market, the easier it will be to make sound selections about which initiatives to fund.

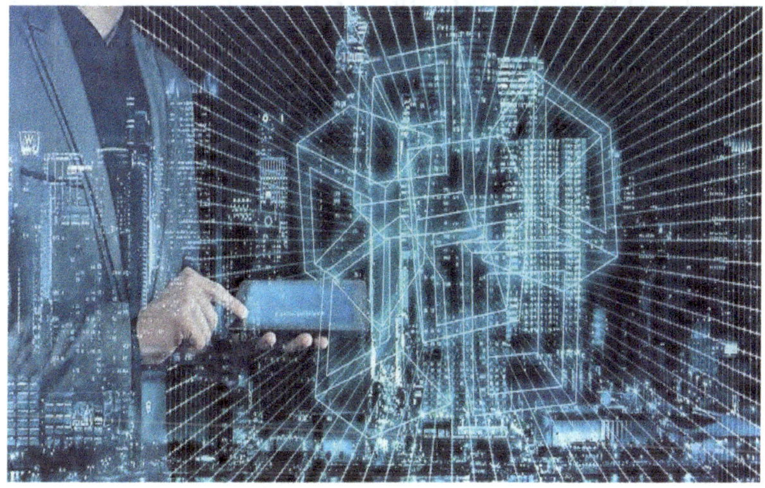

In practise, there are two basic approaches to investing in blockchain technology: cryptocurrencies and everything else. These are not mutually exclusive, and as we have seen with projects such as Ethereum and Ripple, there is frequently some crossover between the two, or the integration of a digital token into a specific blockchain application.

There are busy online marketplaces and exchanges in the cryptocurrency area, with a trading culture comparable to traditional stock exchanges. People swap fiat currency for cryptocurrencies as well as one cryptocurrency for another, hoping to benefit by investing in currencies that they believe will rise in value.

The majority of cryptocurrency exchanges primarily trade in Bitcoin. You nearly always need some Bitcoin to swap in order to purchase into other cryptocurrencies, while some currencies and exchanges allow for a direct conversion between fiat and "altcoins," a common term for cryptocurrencies other than Bitcoin. You can purchase Bitcoin via various online exchanges or from one of the growing number of Bitcoin ATMs present in various locations across the world.

You can opt to trade between different cryptocurrencies actively, or you can simply invest in Bitcoin and/or altcoins that you believe are promising and hold them with the expectation that their value will rise over time. This is one method of participating in what is now the most active ecosystem for blockchain applications. If you're lucky, you might end up as a "early investor" in a technology that explodes in popularity.

Many people have entered the cryptocurrency market with that expectation, especially after hearing about Bitcoin's success. If you are new to blockchain-based digital currencies, you should be aware that this is a highly volatile market. It is not uncommon to see large spikes and declines in value over a few hours; while it is possible to win a lot of money if you play your cards well, it is also possible to lose money.

Being aware of the risks and making wise investments in cryptocurrencies is possibly the quickest way to profit from blockchain technology. It is, without a doubt, the simplest. The notion of mining can be tempting to persons who do not have a lot of money to invest. We've already explored some of the difficulties connected with Bitcoin mining, such as the need to purchase specialist equipment, the high cost of electricity, the requirement for vast computational power, and so on. Starting a Bitcoin mining operation is generally not the greatest idea if you don't have a lot of money.

There are, however, many other cryptocurrencies that can be mined with a far lower barrier to entry. The capacity to earn currencies through mining can be a potential approach to produce passive income through confirming blockchain transactions for people who are ready to learn what it takes to convert a spare computer into a mining rig.

Blockchain technology arose from the cryptocurrency space, and much of the early development of blockchain applications was focused on digital assets and financial transactions. Getting engaged with cryptocurrencies is one popular way to profit from blockchain technology, but it is not the only game in town. As Blockchain makes its way into new industries, a knowledgeable investor can discover a plethora of exciting offshoots that have the potential to grow into large businesses with global significance and take the world by storm. Investing in companies, developers, and technology that are exploring the potential of Blockchain is becoming increasingly popular among everyone from Silicon Valley entrepreneurs to Wall Street executives.

Of all, no one can predict which blockchain-based application will become "the next Google." Any potential investor will undoubtedly face the issue of determining which ventures are over-hyped against which are promising underdogs, which are revolutionary platforms versus cheap knockoffs. While no crystal ball can foretell the future, you may increase your chances of picking a winner by conducting study and asking the correct questions. When determining if a project has a good likelihood of success,

some crucial questions to ask are:

- What issue does the technology address?
- (Does adding a blockchain make sense in this case? Is this the best possible solution?)
- Is this project genuinely working?
- Is it operational and in use, or is it a concept that has yet to be realized?
- How can you be certain that it will actually do what it says if it hasn't been built?

- What is the structure of the Blockchain? (For example, if the founder controls 90% of the network's nodes, what does that indicate about the company?)
- What is their algorithm for reaching a consensus? Proof-of-Work?
- Proof-of-Stake?
- Is there anything else?
- Why did they select this system, and how is it being used?
- Can it be scaled?
- Could this system suit the needs of a huge number of users?
- How does anonymity play a role in this application?
- Is that important?
- Is this platform safe to use?
- How is security ensured?
- Is "trust" present in a centralized body?
- What type of encryption are they employing?

- Is the Blockchain accessible to the public?
- Is the project's code available as open-source?
- (If it isn't, why isn't it?
- When we use this platform, how will we be able to understand how judgments are made, transactions are judged acceptable, and what exactly is being executed?)
- Who is behind this initiative?
- Is the development crew knowledgeable and trustworthy?
- Have they been involved in past failed projects?
- What caused those to fail?
- Are there any other projects that are doing something similar?
- What distinguishes this one as the best?

- Do you have faith in this project?

- Are you looking forward to it?

This is by no means an exhaustive list of questions, but if you are considering investing significant funds in blockchain technology, these concerns are an excellent place to start. With multiple major sectors focusing their attention on blockchain technology, it should come as no surprise that many entrepreneurs have noticed the potential for large money in developing blockchain applications. Needless to say, not all of these applications will be successful, and some appear to be more promising than others. Some initiatives may be wonderful attempts that simply lack the best solution to a common problem, while others may be obvious scams.

Take the time to become acquainted with the blockchain industry's buzzwords and jargon. When a new firm claims to provide a blockchain platform that is "100% scalable," a prudent investor will likely inquire as to how this was accomplished, rather than taking the company's word for it. More often than not, grandiose assertions like "100% scalable" may be closer to "future ambitions" than to current reality.

It is no secret that marketing hype may have a significant impact on how "popular" something becomes. Cryptocurrencies and blockchain-based firms are no exception, and marketing may significantly impact how a participant in this sector is valued. Perhaps a project lives up to the hype, but it's a good idea to approach possible investments in this field with a healthy dose of scepticism. Alternatively, some of the most inventive and exciting blockchain ventures may be smaller start-ups with limited finances, no flashy websites, and little public attention.

Staying informed, looking at a wide range of projects, determining which problems you believe blockchain technology could most successfully answer, and receiving exposure to other points of view will help you acquire an in-depth grasp of the blockchain field. While there are no guarantees when it comes to investing, knowing what to look for can help you make sound selections. Blockchain is still in its early stages, and making wise decisions now has the potential to result in massive gains.

Blockchain Technology's Limitations and Challenges

Understanding the concept of a blockchain is one thing; actually, building one that scales over time, remains secure, and performs in real-world circumstances is quite another. Even if you successfully accomplish all of this, the difficulty of convincing people to invest in and use your technology might be enormous. Those interested in getting involved in the blockchain field should look at some of the potential drawbacks,

problems, and restrictions that blockchain technology now confronts.

- **Speed**

Speed is one of the most difficult difficulties for Bitcoin and other blockchains based on a Proof-of-Work paradigm. Because mining a block is so resource expensive and includes so much trial and error in terms of finding the appropriate nonce to solve a block, each new block takes about 10 minutes to mine.

This not only consumes a large amount of electricity, but it also means that transactions are not validated instantly. In fact, it may take some time for your transaction to move from "pending" to "confirmed." In practice, this makes it difficult to buy things using Bitcoin in many cases. Most individuals do not want to sit in a store for an hour while processing their transaction. Furthermore, most merchants do not want to wait for their money to arrive.

Despite this, the number of merchants willing to accept Bitcoin is increasing on a daily basis. As additional blockchain implementations emerge, alternative transaction and verification speed methods are being developed. Ripple, for example, provides instantaneous transactions, but many critics are concerned about the centralization of the underlying protocol that underpins the technology that allows for such speed.

As a potential investor in a new technology, it is critical to inquire about how this is being addressed and whether security is being sacrificed to increase speed. This is not always the case, but it is something to keep in mind when researching new blockchain systems.

- **Scaling**

Another significant difficulty now confronting blockchain systems is scaling. If you view the Blockchain as a lengthy chain of blocks, you can assume that as more transactions occur and more blocks are added, the chain grows longer and longer.

Many versions of a blockchain are kept and updated over a decentralized network is part of what makes it work. In principle, as a chain grows in length, it will take up more and more space. If a chain became so large that it required a large amount of storage space, people who did not have the space to store the chain would be unable to join in the network. As a result, only massive servers would be able to store the massive chain over time, returning us to the very centralized model that blockchain technology was designed to avoid.

Scaling is a major issue that bitcoin and blockchain inventors are addressing in various ways. The "Lightning Network" is one method that has been proposed as a promising potential solution to the current scaling issues that blockchain applications are experiencing.

The Lightning Network operates by allowing peer-to-peer microtransactions to instantly use blockchain smart contracts, but without adding individual transactions to the main Blockchain. The Lightning Network also supports "atomic swaps" between different blockchains, or from one cryptocurrency to another, as long as both chains support the same cryptographic hash functions. The Lightning Network, which combines the Bitcoin blockchain with its own in-house programming language to manage smart contracts, is one example of a blockchain-based solution to the challenge of blockchain scaling. This is one example of how this technology can create new implementations on top of the old architecture.

- **Quantum computing**

Quantum computers may sound like science fiction, but they are on their way to becoming a reality. Without delving into the "how" of quantum computing, we must consider the "what" of blockchain technology. What does quantum computing mean for us in general, and what does it mean for blockchain technology?

In a word, quantum computing holds the potential of extraordinary speed and power. As of now, we know that blocks are "mined" by a decentralized network of machines that work to validate Bitcoin transactions by completing challenging math problems in exchange for a little amount of Bitcoin. A block is added to the chain once the problem has been rectified and the transaction has been validated.

Quantum computers might be able to tackle these math problems much faster than anything now available. That is the first issue.

The second issue emerges when considering the majority consensus paradigm that rules the Bitcoin system. To change the Blockchain, one would have to change the record on more than half of the copies stored worldwide.

Today, the processing power necessary to do so successfully makes hacking the Blockchain difficult. Quantum computing can change that, however this risk is still theoretical.

CHAPTER 6

The Human Touch:

Or

, The 51% Problem

The capacity to execute transactions in a trustless environment without the need for a "middleman" is one of the key cornerstones of blockchain technology. In layman's terms, we eventually faith in an unbiased mathematical procedure carried out by computers rather than humans. We are assured a level of security that is theoretically as free of human interference as feasible.

Of fact, it is impossible to dismiss humans entirely.

The potential of a decentralized application based on computational verification represents a substantial paradigm change away from a top-down structure and toward a distributed network. When we look at the Bitcoin blockchain, we can see that the consensus model requires a majority of people to agree in order to verify a block. A majority of miners (51%) make up the majority.

What happens if, as mining costs rise in tandem with the Blockchain's expansion, miners pool their power into larger and larger pools? This isn't just a theoretical worry. At the time of writing, it is estimated that two huge mining pools mine about half of all Bitcoin blocks.

To carry out a "51 percent attack," a single entity must supply 51 percent or more of the total Bitcoin network's mining hash rate. This would necessitate an almost incomprehensible amount of computer power, as well as an equally incomprehensible quantity of electricity.

In reality, most countries lack the capacity to carry out a 51 percent onslaught on Bitcoin. It would be extremely tough, but it is not impossible. If this occurred, the attacker would not be able to gain complete control of the network. They would be able to prevent new transactions from being validated, but they would not be able to reverse already recorded transactions, steal Bitcoins from other people's wallets, or produce new Bitcoins at will.

Any decentralized institution created on a similar paradigm will have to deal with the 51 percent problem. Some supporters of Proof-of-Stake consensus argue that it provides better protection against a 51 percent attack.

Blockchains, like all burgeoning industries and new technologies, have hurdles. A new generation of entrepreneurs, developers, and experts is developing in the blockchain arena, and it is a land of opportunity for those who believe in the transformative potential of this technology.

Blockchain Technology's Future

Throughout the course of this book, we've examined a number of fundamental ideas related to blockchain technology. As the world becomes more interconnected through networked technology, and the amount of data we generate expands in both quantity and form, there is a growing demand and opportunity for new organizational structures to handle the interface between digital and material life. The use of a distributed ledger by Blockchain, as well as the potential for constructing decentralized rather than hierarchical systems in a safe, trustless, and open manner, represents a significant step toward reinventing the way many of today's dominating institutions operate.

In the blockchain realm, there are conflicting ideologies, diverse implementations, and a number of obstacles, as with any new technology. Only time will tell if the Bitcoin blockchain will remain the dominant blockchain model and Bitcoin will remain the most popular cryptocurrency. When it comes to reaching the full potential of blockchain technology in terms of enabling institutional transparency, decentralized networks, peer-to-peer transactions, asset management, and much more, there is without a doubt a lot of opportunity for growth. Healthcare, banking, social media, retail, aviation, and manufacturing have all begun to investigate the possibility of merging with blockchain-based systems. Governments, banks, and organizations are already using blockchain technologies to manage transactions, access to public services, and the provision of humanitarian relief.

Whether you are intrigued by the ideological implications of decentralized networks fundamentally altering the landscape of hierarchical organizations on a global scale, or you are an investor looking to get in on the ground floor of the next big thing, blockchain technology is extremely promising.

Blockchain is without a doubt the way of the future. Despite a surge in interest in blockchain technology in recent years, we are still in the early phases of this field. Even if you're new to Blockchain today, you'll most certainly be called a "early adopter" of the most disruptive technology since the Internet's inception in five or 10 years.

Conclusion

I'd want to thank you for purchasing this book, and I applaud you for taking the time to learn about the game-changing blockchain technology.

I hope this brief read has given you a basic grasp of bitcoin and the Blockchain, piqued your interest, and piqued your desire to do more research and begin your road toward sovereignty.

The following stage is to become involved in the message boards and with the resources described in this book.

Finally, if you loved this book, I'd appreciate it if you could write a review on Amazon.

It will be gratefully received.

Thank you, and best wishes.